# Cybersecurity Unlocked: Essential Tactics to Detect, Prevent, and Manage Modern Threats

By
Eric Fennimore

# Disclaimer

Copyright © by Eric Fennimore 2024. All rights reserved.

Before this document is duplicated or reproduced in any manner, the publisher's consent must be gained. Therefore, the contents within can neither be stored electronically, transferred, nor kept in a database. Neither in Part nor full can the document be copied, scanned, faxed, or retained without approval from the publisher or creator.

# Table of Contents

Disclaimer 2
About The Author 4
About The Book 6
Introduction 8
Chapter 1 - The Digital Battlefield : Understanding Modern Cyber Threats 16
Chapter 2 - The Human Firewall : Strengthening Your First Line of Defense 28
Chapter 3 - Fortress in the Cloud: Securing Remote and Hybrid Work Environments 39
Chapter 4 - Hunting the Invisible: Advanced Threat Detection Techniques 51
Chapter 5 - The Cyber Resilience Playbook: Preparing for the Inevitable 62
Chapter 6 - Guardians of the Grid: Safeguarding Critical Infrastructure 73
Chapter 7 - Future-Proofing Cybersecurity: Trends and Technologies to Watch 86
Appendix 99

# About The Author

Eric Fennimore is a seasoned cybersecurity expert with over two decades of experience safeguarding organizations from the ever-evolving landscape of digital threats. Known for his innovative approach to problem-solving, Eric has worked with Fortune 500 companies, government agencies, and startups, helping them build resilient systems to counter cyberattacks.

As a passionate advocate for cybersecurity awareness, Eric has dedicated his career to demystifying complex security concepts, making them accessible to individuals and businesses alike. His ability to blend technical expertise with practical advice has earned him a reputation as a trusted voice in the cybersecurity community.

In Cybersecurity Unlocked: Essential Tactics to Detect, Prevent, and Manage Modern Threats, Eric draws on his vast experience to provide readers with actionable strategies to protect their digital lives. Whether you're a business owner, IT professional, or simply someone looking to secure your online presence, Eric's insights will empower you to navigate the digital world with confidence.

When he's not writing or consulting, Eric enjoys exploring emerging technologies, mentoring the next generation of cybersecurity professionals, and spending time with his family.

## About The Book

In Cybersecurity Unlocked, Eric Fennimore delivers a masterclass on navigating the perilous world of modern cyber threats. With a perfect blend of technical expertise and accessible language, this book demystifies the complexities of cybersecurity, making it an invaluable resource for both seasoned IT professionals and everyday users seeking to safeguard their digital lives.

Fennimore's ability to break down intricate concepts into actionable insights is unparalleled. From understanding the anatomy of cyberattacks to implementing robust prevention strategies, every chapter is packed with practical advice. The real-world case studies add a compelling dimension, showcasing how these tactics have been applied to thwart cybercriminals.

What sets Cybersecurity Unlocked apart is its forward-thinking approach. Fennimore doesn't just focus on current threats; he prepares readers for the evolving landscape of cyber risks, offering strategies to stay ahead of the curve. The inclusion of tips for businesses, individuals, and even non-technical audiences ensures that no one is left behind in the fight against cybercrime.

Whether you're a tech-savvy professional or someone just beginning to understand the importance of cybersecurity, this book is a must-read. Eric Fennimore has crafted a definitive guide that is as engaging as it is educational. Cybersecurity Unlocked is not just a book, it's a critical tool for thriving in the digital age.

Rating: 5/5 – A compelling and indispensable guide for anyone navigating the digital world.

# Introduction

In a world increasingly driven by technology, the line between convenience and vulnerability has become alarmingly thin. The digital revolution has transformed how we live, work, and interact, creating unprecedented opportunities and risks. Every click, swipe, and login carries the potential to unlock doors to innovation or open gateways for cybercriminals. This duality underscores the critical need for a robust understanding of cybersecurity.

Cybersecurity Unlocked: Essential Tactics to Detect, Prevent, and Manage Modern Threats is your comprehensive guide to navigating the complex and ever-evolving digital landscape. Whether you are a seasoned IT professional, a business leader, or an everyday internet user, this book equips you with the knowledge and strategies needed to stay ahead of cyber threats.

## **Why Cybersecurity Matters**

In today's interconnected world, cybersecurity is no longer optional; it is a necessity. The rapid proliferation of smart devices, cloud computing, and remote work has expanded the attack surface for malicious actors. Cyberattacks are no longer confined to large corporations or government institutions; they affect individuals, small businesses, and even critical infrastructure.

Consider this: in 2023 alone, global cybercrime costs were estimated to exceed $8 trillion, with ransomware attacks occurring every 11 seconds. These staggering numbers highlight the urgent need for proactive measures to safeguard sensitive data and systems. Yet, despite the growing threat, many remain unaware of the vulnerabilities lurking in their digital lives.

This book aims to bridge that gap. It demystifies cybersecurity, breaking down complex concepts into actionable insights. From identifying phishing scams to implementing advanced threat detection systems, you will learn how to build a resilient defense against cyber adversaries.

**The Scope of Modern Threats**

The threats we face today are more sophisticated than ever. Cybercriminals are leveraging artificial intelligence, machine learning, and automation to launch highly targeted attacks. Social engineering schemes exploit human psychology, while advanced persistent threats (APTs) infiltrate networks, remaining undetected for months or even years.

This book explores the wide spectrum of modern threats, including:

**Phishing and Social Engineering:** Manipulative tactics that trick individuals into divulging sensitive information.

**Ransomware:** Malicious software that locks systems and demands payment for their release.

**Zero-Day Exploits:** Attacks that take advantage of vulnerabilities before they are patched.

**Insider Threats:** Risks posed by employees, contractors, or trusted third parties.

**Supply Chain Attacks:** Breaches targeting vendors and suppliers to compromise larger networks.

Understanding these threats is the first step toward effective prevention and mitigation.

## A Practical Approach to Cybersecurity

What sets this book apart is its focus on practicality. Cybersecurity is not just about technology; it is about people, processes, and strategies. Each chapter is designed to provide clear, actionable advice that you can implement immediately.

Key topics covered include:

**Building a Cybersecurity Framework:** Learn how to create a structured approach to managing cyber risks.

**Incident Response Planning:** Develop a step-by-step plan for detecting, responding to, and recovering from cyber incidents.

**Threat Intelligence:** Understand how to gather and analyze information about potential threats to stay ahead of attackers.

**Personal Cyber Hygiene:** Discover simple habits to protect yourself from online threats.

**Emerging Technologies:** Explore how innovations like blockchain, AI, and quantum computing are shaping the future of cybersecurity.

By combining technical expertise with practical advice, this book empowers readers to take control of their digital security.

## Who This Book Is For

Cybersecurity affects everyone, regardless of their background or profession. This book is designed for a diverse audience, including:

**IT Professionals:** Gain advanced insights into threat detection, prevention, and mitigation.

**Business Leaders:** Understand the importance of cybersecurity in protecting organizational assets and maintaining customer trust.

**Everyday Users:** Learn simple yet effective ways to safeguard personal information and devices.

Whether you are securing a multinational corporation or protecting your home network, this book provides the tools you need to succeed.

## A Call to Action

The battle against cyber threats is not fought in isolation. It requires a collective effort, from governments and businesses to individuals and communities. As you delve into the pages of this book, remember that cybersecurity is not a destination but a journey. It is an ongoing commitment to vigilance, education, and adaptation.

Cybersecurity Unlocked invites you to take that journey. By understanding the tactics, technologies, and strategies outlined in this book, you will be better equipped to detect, prevent, and manage modern threats. Together, we can create a safer digital future for everyone.

Welcome to the world of cybersecurity unlocked.

# Chapter 1: The Digital Battlefield: Understanding Modern Cyber Threats

In the modern era, cyberspace has evolved into a vast and dynamic battlefield. Organizations, governments, and individuals face an ever-growing array of cyber threats, fueled by technological advancements and the interconnected nature of our world. To navigate this digital battlefield effectively, it is crucial to understand the evolving landscape of cyber risks and the sophisticated tactics employed by attackers.

## The Evolving Cyber Threat Landscape

### 1. The Rise of Sophisticated Attackers

Cybercriminals today are no longer lone hackers operating in isolation. They are often part of well-organized groups, including state-sponsored actors, hacktivists, and cybercrime syndicates. These groups leverage advanced tools, artificial intelligence (AI), and machine learning (ML) to launch highly targeted attacks.

For instance, ransomware attacks have shifted from random campaigns to "big game hunting," where attackers specifically target high-value organizations. The Colonial Pipeline attack in 2021 highlighted how critical infrastructure can become a prime target, causing widespread disruption and financial loss.

## 2. The Expanding Attack Surface

The proliferation of connected devices, or the Internet of Things (IoT), has significantly expanded the attack surface. Smart homes, wearable devices, and industrial control systems are now interconnected, creating more entry points for attackers. Each device added to a network is a potential vulnerability.

## 3. The Human Factor

Despite advancements in technology, humans remain the weakest link in cybersecurity. Phishing attacks, social engineering, and insider threats exploit human psychology to bypass sophisticated security measures. The 2020 Twitter hack, where attackers manipulated employees to gain access to high-profile accounts, underscores the importance of addressing human vulnerabilities.

## 4. The Speed of Innovation

As organizations adopt cloud computing, artificial intelligence, and blockchain, attackers are quick to exploit vulnerabilities in these emerging technologies. Zero-day exploits attacks that occur before a vulnerability is patched are becoming increasingly common, leaving organizations scrambling to mitigate damage.

## Tactics Used by Modern Cyber Attackers

### 1. Social Engineering

Social engineering remains one of the most effective tools in an attacker's arsenal. By manipulating emotions like fear, urgency, or curiosity, attackers trick victims into revealing sensitive information or performing actions that compromise security. Common social engineering tactics include:

**Phishing:** Fraudulent emails designed to steal credentials or deploy malware.

**Vishing:** Voice phishing, where attackers impersonate trusted entities over the phone.

**Smishing:** SMS-based phishing, exploiting the trust placed in text messages.

## 2. Ransomware Attacks
Ransomware has evolved into a lucrative business model for cybercriminals. Attackers encrypt an organization's data and demand payment for its release. In some cases, they also threaten to leak sensitive data if the ransom is not paid, a tactic known as "double extortion."

## 3. Advanced Persistent Threats (APTs)
APTs are long-term, targeted attacks often orchestrated by nation-states or well-funded groups. These attackers infiltrate networks, remain undetected for extended periods, and extract valuable data. The SolarWinds attack, which compromised multiple government agencies and corporations, exemplifies the danger of APTs.

## 4. Malware

Malware, or malicious software, comes in various forms, including viruses, worms, trojans, and spyware. Modern malware is designed to evade detection by traditional antivirus programs and can propagate rapidly across networks.

## 5. Distributed Denial of Service (DDoS) Attacks

DDoS attacks overwhelm a target's servers with excessive traffic, rendering services unavailable. These attacks are often used to disrupt operations, distract security teams, or as a precursor to more invasive breaches.

## 6. Exploitation of Supply Chains

Supply chain attacks target third-party vendors or software providers to infiltrate larger organizations. By compromising a trusted partner, attackers gain indirect access to their ultimate target. The 2020 SolarWinds breach demonstrated how devastating supply chain attacks can be.

## 7. Exfiltration of Data

Attackers often seek to steal sensitive information for financial gain, espionage, or blackmail. Personal data, intellectual property, and trade secrets are valuable commodities on the dark web.

## The Impact of Cyber Threats

Cyber threats have far-reaching consequences that extend beyond financial losses. They can erode trust, damage reputations, and disrupt critical services. For individuals, a data breach can lead to identity theft, financial ruin, and emotional distress. For organizations, the fallout includes regulatory penalties, legal liabilities, and loss of customer confidence.

## 1. Economic Costs

The global cost of cybercrime is projected to reach $10.5 trillion annually by 2025, according to Cybersecurity Ventures. These costs include direct losses, recovery expenses, and investments in improved security measures.

## 2. **National Security Risks**

State-sponsored attacks often target government agencies, military operations, and critical infrastructure. Cyber warfare has become a key component of modern conflict, with nations using digital tools to disrupt adversaries and gain strategic advantages.

## 3. **Disruption of Critical Services**

Healthcare systems, power grids, and transportation networks are increasingly targeted by cybercriminals. A ransomware attack on a hospital, for example, can delay critical medical procedures and put lives at risk.

## 4. **Psychological Impact**

The psychological toll of cyberattacks is often overlooked. Victims may experience anxiety, stress, and a loss of trust in digital systems. Organizations may also face internal conflicts and employee dissatisfaction following a breach.

## Defending Against Cyber Threats

### 1. Adopting a Proactive Mindset

Cybersecurity is no longer a reactive endeavor. Organizations must adopt a proactive approach, identifying vulnerabilities and mitigating risks before they can be exploited. This includes conducting regular security assessments, penetration testing, and threat modeling.

### 2. Implementing Zero Trust Architecture

Zero Trust is a security model that assumes no user or device is trustworthy by default. It emphasizes strict access controls, continuous monitoring, and verification of every user and device attempting to access a network.

### 3. Investing in Threat Intelligence

Threat intelligence provides insights into emerging threats, enabling organizations to anticipate and counter attacks. By analyzing data from various sources, security teams can identify patterns and trends in attacker behavior.

## 4. Strengthening Endpoint Security

Endpoints, such as laptops, smartphones, and IoT devices, are common entry points for attackers. Robust endpoint security solutions, including antivirus software, firewalls, and device management tools, are essential for protecting these vulnerabilities.

## 5. Enhancing Employee Awareness

Human error is a leading cause of security breaches. Comprehensive training programs can help employees recognize phishing attempts, practice safe online behaviors, and understand their role in maintaining cybersecurity.

## 6. Incident Response Planning

Even with the best defenses, breaches can occur. An effective incident response plan ensures a swift and coordinated reaction, minimizing damage and facilitating recovery. This includes clear communication protocols, predefined roles, and regular drills to test the plan's effectiveness.

## 7. Collaboration and Information Sharing

Cybersecurity is a collective effort. Organizations, governments, and industry groups must collaborate to share threat intelligence, best practices, and lessons learned. Public-private partnerships are particularly valuable in addressing large-scale threats.

## The Road Ahead

As technology continues to evolve, so too will the tactics of cyber attackers. Artificial intelligence, quantum computing, and the metaverse are just a few of the innovations that will reshape the digital battlefield. To stay ahead, organizations must embrace a culture of continuous learning, adaptability, and resilience.

The stakes in the digital battlefield are high, but by understanding modern cyber threats and adopting robust defense strategies, we can navigate this complex terrain and safeguard our digital future.

# Chapter 2: The Human Firewall: Strengthening Your First Line of Defense

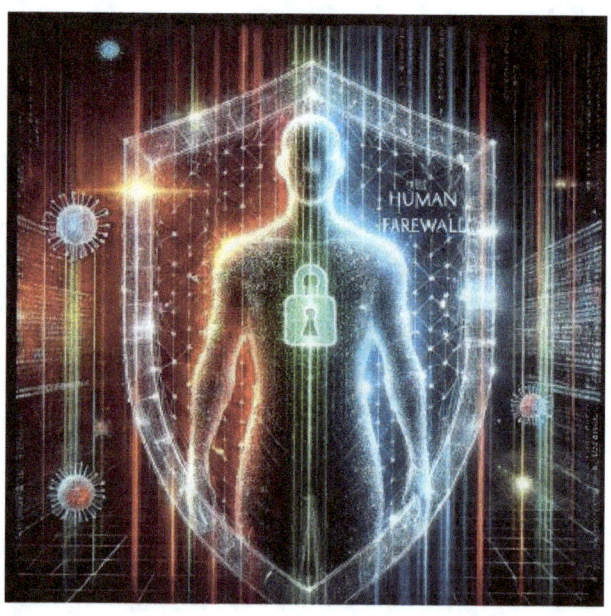

In the digital age, organizations face a relentless onslaught of cyber threats, ranging from phishing emails to sophisticated ransomware attacks. While advanced technologies like firewalls, antivirus software, and intrusion detection systems play a critical role in safeguarding data, the human element often remains the weakest link. However, with the right training and awareness, employees can transform into the strongest line of defense—the human firewall.

## **The Role of the Human Firewall**

A human firewall refers to employees who are trained and vigilant against cyber threats, acting as the first line of defense in identifying and mitigating potential breaches. Unlike automated systems, humans can apply judgment and context to situations, making them uniquely capable of detecting suspicious activity that might bypass traditional defenses.

However, without proper training and awareness, employees can inadvertently become enablers of cyberattacks. Studies show that human error is responsible for over 80% of data breaches. This underscores the importance of cultivating a culture of cybersecurity awareness within an organization.

## Why Employee Awareness Matters

### 1. The Rise of Social Engineering Attacks

Cybercriminals increasingly rely on social engineering tactics, such as phishing, baiting, and pretexting, to manipulate individuals into divulging sensitive information. These attacks exploit human psychology rather than technical vulnerabilities, making untrained employees prime targets.

### 2. Phishing Emails

One of the most common attack vectors is still phishing. A well-crafted phishing email can deceive even tech-savvy individuals into clicking malicious links or sharing login credentials. Educated employees can recognize red flags, such as unusual sender addresses or urgent requests for personal information.

3. **Weak Password Practices**

Despite advances in authentication technology, weak or reused passwords continue to compromise security. Employees must understand the importance of creating strong, unique passwords and using tools like password managers.

4. **Shadow IT Risks**

Employees often use unauthorized software or devices for convenience, unaware of the security risks. Training can highlight the dangers of shadow IT and encourage adherence to company policies.

**Building an Effective Human Firewall**

To transform employees into proactive defenders of organizational security, businesses must implement comprehensive awareness and training programs.

**1. Cybersecurity Training Programs**

Regular training sessions should cover:

- Identifying phishing emails and social engineering tactics.
- Best practices for password security.
- Safe internet browsing habits.
- Recognizing and reporting suspicious activity.

Training should be interactive and engaging, incorporating simulations, quizzes, and real-world scenarios.

## 2. Phishing Simulations

Conducting simulated phishing attacks can help employees practice identifying threats in a controlled environment. These exercises not only test awareness but also provide valuable feedback for improvement.

## 3. Role-Specific Training

Different roles within an organization face unique cybersecurity challenges. For instance, finance teams may be targeted with invoice fraud, while IT staff must guard against insider threats. Tailored training ensures relevance and effectiveness.

### 4. Gamification and Rewards
Introducing gamification elements, such as leaderboards and rewards for spotting phishing attempts, can make training more engaging and encourage participation.

### 5. Clear Reporting Channels
Employees should know how and where to report suspicious activity without fear of reprisal. Clear reporting channels foster a sense of responsibility and collaboration.

### 6. Regular Updates and Communication
The cybersecurity landscape evolves rapidly. Regular updates, newsletters, and workshops keep employees informed about emerging threats and new best practices.

## Cultivating a Cybersecurity Culture

Building a human firewall requires more than just training; it demands a cultural shift where cybersecurity becomes an integral part of daily operations.

## 1. Leadership Commitment

Leaders must set the tone by prioritizing cybersecurity and participating in training initiatives. Their involvement reinforces the importance of vigilance at all levels.

## 2. Empowering Employees

Employees should feel empowered to take ownership of cybersecurity. This includes fostering an environment where questions are encouraged and mistakes are treated as learning opportunities.

## 3. Incorporating Cybersecurity into Onboarding

Cybersecurity training should begin during the onboarding process. New hires should understand their role in protecting the organization from day one.

**4. Promoting Collaboration**
Cybersecurity is a shared responsibility. Encouraging collaboration between departments ensures a unified approach to threat detection and response.

## Measuring the Effectiveness of the Human Firewall

To ensure the success of awareness and training programs, organizations must regularly assess their human firewall's effectiveness.

**1. Metrics and KPIs**
Key performance indicators (KPIs) can include:
- Reduction in successful phishing attempts.
- Number of reported suspicious activities.
- Employee participation in training sessions.

**2. Surveys and Feedback**

Collecting employee feedback helps identify gaps in training and areas for improvement.

### 3. Incident Response Drills
Simulated incidents, such as ransomware attacks or data breaches, can test the organization's overall preparedness and highlight weaknesses in the human firewall.

### The Cost of Neglecting the Human Element

Failing to invest in employee awareness and training can have severe consequences, including:

**Financial Losses:** Data breaches can result in hefty fines, legal fees, and loss of revenue.

**Reputational Damage:** A breach can erode customer trust and tarnish the organization's reputation.

**Operational Disruption:** Cyberattacks can disrupt business operations, leading to downtime and productivity loss.

**Success Stories:** Organizations with Strong Human Firewalls

Many organizations have successfully reduced cyber threats by prioritizing employee awareness. For instance:

- A global financial institution reported a 60% drop in phishing-related incidents after implementing regular training and simulations.
- A healthcare provider avoided a ransomware attack when an alert employee recognized and reported a suspicious email.

## Conclusion

In the battle against cyber threats, technology alone is not enough. Employees are the first line of defense, and their vigilance can mean the difference between a thwarted attack and a devastating breach. By investing in awareness, training, and a culture of cybersecurity, organizations can transform their workforce into a formidable human firewall, safeguarding their assets and reputation in an increasingly digital world.

By strengthening this critical line of defense, businesses not only protect themselves but also empower their employees to be active participants in the fight against cybercrime.

# Chapter 3: Fortress in the Cloud: Securing Remote and Hybrid Work Environments

As businesses adapt to the demands of remote and hybrid work environments, the challenge of securing decentralized systems and data becomes increasingly critical. While remote work offers flexibility and productivity gains, it also expands the attack surface for cybercriminals. This chapter explores strategies to build a robust "fortress in the cloud," ensuring data integrity and system security in a distributed workplace.

## The Decentralized Challenge

The shift to remote and hybrid work has introduced vulnerabilities that traditional security models struggle to address. Employees now access sensitive data from various locations, devices, and networks. This decentralization demands a rethinking of security strategies to accommodate:

**1. Inconsistent Network Security:** Employees often use home or public Wi-Fi, which may lack robust security measures.

**2. Personal Devices:** The use of personal laptops or smartphones introduces risks due to weaker security protocols.

**3. Cloud Reliance:** Cloud-based tools and platforms, while convenient, require vigilant monitoring to prevent unauthorized access.

**4. Insider Threats:** A dispersed workforce increases the difficulty of detecting insider threats, whether intentional or accidental.

To address these challenges, organizations must adopt a layered approach to security, leveraging advanced technologies and promoting a culture of cybersecurity awareness.

## Zero Trust Architecture: The Core of Remote Security

Zero Trust Architecture (ZTA) is a paradigm shift in cybersecurity that operates on the principle of "never trust, always verify." This approach assumes that threats can originate from both inside and outside the network. Implementing ZTA involves:

**1. Identity and Access Management (IAM):**

- Enforce multi-factor authentication (MFA) for all users.
- Use role-based access control (RBAC) to limit data access to what is necessary for each role.

**2. Network Segmentation:**
- In order to prevent possible breaches, divide the network into segments.
- Restrict lateral movement by isolating critical systems.

**3. Continuous Monitoring:**

- Deploy tools to monitor user behavior and detect anomalies.
- Use AI-driven analytics to identify potential threats in real time.

**Securing the Endpoint**

Endpoints, such as laptops, tablets, and smartphones, are the first line of defense in a remote work environment. Securing these devices involves:

### 1. Endpoint Detection and Response (EDR):

- Use EDR solutions to monitor, detect, and respond to threats on endpoints.
- Implement automated responses to isolate compromised devices.

### 2. Device Management:

- Require all devices to meet minimum security standards, including antivirus software and encryption.
- Use Mobile Device Management (MDM) tools to enforce policies and remotely wipe lost or stolen devices.

### 3. Regular Updates and Patching:

- Make sure that programs and operating systems are updated frequently.
- Automate patch management to reduce vulnerabilities.

**Securing Cloud Infrastructure**

Cloud platforms are central to remote work, offering scalability and collaboration tools. However, they also require robust security measures:

**1. Cloud Access Security Brokers (CASBs):**

- Deploy CASBs to monitor and control access to cloud applications.
- Enforce policies such as data loss prevention (DLP) and encryption.

**2. Shared Responsibility Model:**

- Understand how security responsibilities are divided between the cloud provider and the organization.
- Implement additional security measures to complement the provider's offerings.

## 3. **Encryption:**

- To avoid unwanted access, encrypt data while it's in transit and at rest.
- Use end-to-end encryption for sensitive communications.

## **The Human Factor: Building a Cyber-Aware Culture**

Technology alone cannot secure remote and hybrid work environments. Workers play an important role in maintaining security. Organizations should:

## 1. **Conduct Regular Training:**

- Workers should be trained to spot phishing attempts and other forms of social engineering.
- Provide clear guidelines for handling sensitive data.

## 2. **Simulate Cyberattacks:**
- Conduct phishing simulations to assess and improve employee awareness.
- Use the results to tailor training programs.

## 3. **Establish Clear Policies:**
- Create policies for acceptable use of devices and networks.
- Communicate the consequences of policy violations.

## **Incident Response in a Decentralized Workplace**

To lessen the effects of security breaches, a strong incident response plan is crucial. In a remote work environment, this plan should include:

## 1. Decentralized Detection:

Use distributed monitoring tools to detect threats across all endpoints and networks.

## 2. Rapid Communication:

- Establish clear channels for reporting incidents.
- Use encrypted communication tools to share sensitive information during a breach.

## 3. Recovery and Continuity:

- Maintain regular backups of critical data and test restoration techniques.
- Develop a business continuity plan to maintain operations during an incident.

## The Role of Artificial Intelligence and Machine Learning

AI and machine learning (ML) are powerful tools for securing remote and hybrid work environments. Their applications include:

### 1. Threat Detection:

- Use ML algorithms to analyze patterns and identify potential threats.
- Detects anomalies in user behavior that may indicate compromised accounts.

### 2. Automated Responses:

Deploy AI-driven tools to respond to threats in real time, such as isolating infected devices.

### 3. Predictive Analysis:

Leverage AI to predict potential vulnerabilities and address them proactively.

### Future-Proofing Remote Work Security

The evolution of remote and hybrid work is ongoing, and security strategies must adapt to emerging threats. Future-proofing involves:

1. **Investing in Emerging Technologies:**

    - Explore blockchain for secure data sharing.
    - Use quantum encryption to protect against advanced cyberattacks.

2. **Regular Audits:**

To find and fix vulnerabilities, do regular security audits.

3. **Fostering Collaboration:**

Partner with industry peers and government agencies to share threat intelligence.

To conclude;
A multifaceted strategy that incorporates cutting-edge technologies, strong regulations,

and employee knowledge is needed to secure remote and hybrid work settings. By adopting strategies such as Zero Trust Architecture, endpoint security, and cloud protection, organizations can build a "fortress in the cloud" to safeguard their data and systems. As the workplace continues to evolve, proactive and adaptive security measures will be the cornerstone of success in a decentralized world.

# Chapter 4: Hunting the Invisible: Advanced Threat Detection Techniques

In the ever-evolving landscape of cybersecurity, the most dangerous threats are often the ones you cannot see. These invisible threats, hidden vulnerabilities, zero-day exploits, and advanced persistent threats (APTs) are crafted to evade traditional detection systems. To combat these dangers, organizations must adopt advanced threat detection techniques and tools that go beyond the conventional. This chapter explores cutting-edge methodologies and technologies for identifying and neutralizing hidden vulnerabilities, providing you with the knowledge to stay one step ahead of attackers.

**The Nature of Invisible Threats**

Invisible threats are designed to blend into the digital ecosystem, avoiding detection through obfuscation, encryption, and sophisticated evasion techniques. These threats often exploit:

**1. Zero-Day Vulnerabilities:** Flaws in software or hardware that are unknown to the vendor and therefore unpatched.

**2. Fileless Malware:** Malicious code that operates in memory rather than being written to disk, making it harder to detect.

**3. Advanced Persistent Threats (APTs):** Long-term, targeted attacks often backed by nation-states or organized cybercriminal groups.

To effectively hunt these threats, cybersecurity professionals must adopt proactive and adaptive strategies.

## Advanced Threat Detection Techniques

## 1. Behavioral Analytics and Anomaly Detection

Traditional signature-based detection systems are inadequate for identifying novel threats. Behavioral analytics focuses on identifying deviations from normal activity.

**User and Entity Behavior Analytics (UEBA):** UEBA systems establish a baseline of normal behavior for users and devices. Any deviation, such as unusual login times or data transfers, triggers an alert.

**Machine Learning Models:** Advanced machine learning algorithms analyze vast datasets to identify patterns indicative of malicious activity, even if the exact threat is unknown.

**Example:** A machine learning system detects an employee accessing sensitive files at 3 a.m., an unusual behavior that could indicate compromised credentials.

## 2. Threat Intelligence Integration

Threat intelligence platforms aggregate data from multiple sources, providing insights into emerging threats. These platforms enable organizations to:

**Correlate Events:** By comparing internal activity with external threat intelligence, organizations can identify potential compromises.

**Predict Attacks:** Analyzing patterns in threat data helps anticipate and mitigate attacks before they occur.

**Tool Highlight:** MITRE ATT&CK Framework offers a comprehensive knowledge base of adversary tactics and techniques, aiding in threat detection and response planning.

### 3. Endpoint Detection and Response (EDR)

Endpoints are often the weakest link in cybersecurity. EDR tools provide continuous monitoring and response capabilities, including:

**Real-Time Threat Detection:** Identifying suspicious processes or behaviors on endpoints.

**Automated Response:** Isolating infected devices to prevent lateral movement within the network.

**Example:** An EDR tool detects a fileless malware attack leveraging PowerShell and immediately terminates the process.

## 4. Deception Technology

Deception technology involves deploying decoys and traps to lure attackers, diverting them from critical assets and gathering intelligence.

**Honeypots:** Simulated systems designed to attract attackers.

**Honeytokens:** Fake credentials or data embedded in the system to alert administrators when accessed.

**Real-World Use:** A honeypot mimicking a database server detects an attacker probing for vulnerabilities, enabling security teams to trace the source.

### 5. Network Traffic Analysis (NTA)

Monitoring network traffic is crucial for identifying hidden threats. NTA tools analyze data flows for anomalies, such as:

**Unusual Data Transfers:** Large outbound data flows could indicate data exfiltration.

**Command and Control Communication:** Detecting traffic to known malicious domains or IPs.

**Tool Highlight:** Zeek (formerly Bro) is an open-source NTA tool that provides detailed insights into network activity.

## 6. Threat Hunting

Threat hunting involves actively searching for threats that have bypassed automated defenses. It is a proactive approach that combines human expertise with advanced tools.

**Hypothesis-Driven Hunting:** Analysts form hypotheses based on threat intelligence and test them against system data.

**Hunting Queries:** Using tools like Splunk or Elastic Security to query logs for indicators of compromise (IOCs).

**Case Study:** A threat hunter identifies a compromised system by correlating unusual login attempts with known malicious IP addresses.

## Cutting-Edge Tools for Threat Detection

### 1. SIEM (Security Information and Event Management)

SIEM systems collect and analyze log data from across the network, providing centralized visibility and alerting capabilities.

Popular Tools: Splunk, IBM QRadar, and ArcSight.

### 2. SOAR (Security Orchestration, Automation, and Response)

SOAR platforms automate threat response workflows, reducing the time to contain incidents.

**Example:** A SOAR system automatically quarantines a compromised endpoint after detecting suspicious activity.

### 3. AI-Powered Tools

Artificial intelligence enhances threat detection by analyzing complex datasets and identifying subtle patterns.

**Example:** Darktrace uses AI to detect and respond to threats in real time, even in previously unseen scenarios.

## Neutralizing Hidden Vulnerabilities

Identifying threats is only half the battle; effective mitigation strategies are equally critical.

### 1. Patch Management

Regularly updating software and systems eliminates known vulnerabilities. Automated patch management tools streamline this process.

### 2. Access Controls

Implementing the principle of least privilege minimizes the potential impact of a breach.

### 3. Incident Response Plans

A well-defined incident response plan ensures quick and effective action when threats are detected.

### The Future of Threat Detection

As cyber threats continue to evolve, so must detection techniques. Emerging trends include:

**Quantum Computing:** While a potential threat to encryption, quantum technology could also enhance threat detection.

**Behavioral Biometrics:** Using unique behavioral patterns, such as typing speed or mouse movements, to detect compromised accounts.

**Blockchain for Security:** Leveraging blockchain technology for secure and tamper-proof logging of events.

**To conclude;**
Hunting the invisible requires a combination of advanced tools, proactive strategies, and continuous learning. By leveraging behavioral analytics, threat intelligence, EDR, and other cutting-edge techniques, organizations can identify and neutralize hidden vulnerabilities before they cause harm. In the high-stakes world of cybersecurity, staying ahead of attackers is not just an advantage, it is a necessity.

# Chapter 5: The Cyber Resilience Playbook: Preparing for the Inevitable

In today's hyper-connected world, the question is not if a cyberattack will happen, but when it will happen. Cybersecurity breaches are no longer rare occurrences; they are a constant threat that organizations must prepare for. Despite best efforts to prevent attacks, the reality is that no system is entirely immune. Cyber resilience is quite important here. It's not just about defending against cyberattacks, but also about preparing to respond effectively when they occur. In this chapter, we will explore how to build a robust incident response plan that minimizes damage and ensures swift recovery from cyberattacks.

## 1. Understanding Cyber Resilience

Cyber resilience is the ability to continuously deliver the intended outcome despite adverse cyber events. It's about creating a strategy that balances proactive defense, incident response, and recovery. A resilient organization not only has strong cybersecurity measures in place but also the ability to quickly detect, respond to, and recover from attacks with minimal disruption.

The key elements of cyber resilience include:

**Prevention:** Protecting systems from attacks through strong security measures.

**Detection:** Identifying potential threats early through monitoring and alert systems.

**Response:** Having a structured plan to manage and mitigate the impact of attacks.

**Recovery:** Ensuring that critical systems and data can be restored quickly to minimize downtime.

While prevention is essential, the inevitability of cyberattacks makes response and recovery just as important.

## 2. Building a Robust Incident Response Plan

An incident response plan (IRP) is a well-structured approach that organizations use to respond to and manage the aftermath of a cybersecurity incident. A good IRP minimizes the impact of the incident, ensures quick recovery, and helps the organization learn from the attack to improve future defenses. Here's how to build an effective IRP:

## a) Define Roles and Responsibilities

The first step in crafting a successful incident response plan is to clearly define roles and responsibilities. This ensures that everyone knows what to do when an attack occurs. Typically, an incident response team (IRT) should include the following roles:

**Incident Response Manager:** Oversees the entire incident response process and ensures that all actions are aligned with the organization's goals.

**Security Analysts:** Responsible for identifying, analyzing, and containing the threat.

**IT and Systems Administrators:** Help with the technical aspects of the response, such as isolating affected systems and restoring backups.

**Legal and Compliance Officers:** Ensure that the organization complies with relevant laws and regulations, such as data breach notification requirements.

**Public Relations and Communications:** Handle external communications, including notifying customers, stakeholders, and the public, as well as managing the organization's reputation.

**Executive Leadership:** Provides strategic direction and ensures that the response is aligned with the organization's overall goals.

**b) Establish Clear Communication Channels**

Effective communication is crucial during a cyberattack. Clearly define the channels of communication for internal and external stakeholders. Internally, ensure that the incident response team can quickly share information and coordinate actions. Externally, determine how and when to communicate with customers, regulatory bodies, and the media.

Develop templates for public statements, press releases, and customer notifications to ensure consistency and accuracy. The last thing you want during a crisis is confusion about what to say and when to say it.

## c) Identify Critical Assets and Data

Not all assets are created equal. When preparing for an attack, it's essential to know which systems, data, and applications are most critical to the organization's operations. This will help prioritize incident response efforts and minimize disruption.

For example, an e-commerce company might prioritize customer payment systems and inventory management software, while a healthcare organization would focus on patient data and medical records. Identifying these critical assets in advance allows the response team to focus on preserving and restoring the most vital components first.

## d) Develop Incident Response Procedures

The heart of any incident response plan is the set of procedures that guide the response team through the various stages of an attack. These stages typically include:

**I. <u>Preparation</u>:** This phase involves planning and training, ensuring that all systems are in place to detect, respond to, and recover from an incident. Regularly update your plan and conduct tabletop exercises to simulate real-world scenarios.

**II. <u>Identification</u>:** Early detection of an incident is key to minimizing damage. Utilize security monitoring tools, intrusion detection systems (IDS), and threat intelligence feeds to identify suspicious activity. The faster you can identify the attack, the faster you can respond.

**III. <u>Containment</u>:** Once an attack is identified, the next step is to contain it. This may involve isolating affected systems, blocking malicious traffic, or taking systems offline temporarily.

The goal is to prevent the attack from spreading and causing further damage.

**IV. Eradication:** After containment, the focus shifts to eliminating the root cause of the attack. This could entail deleting malware, fixing security flaws, or resetting compromised login credentials. Ensure that all traces of the attack are removed before moving on to recovery.

**V. Recovery:** The recovery phase involves restoring systems and data to normal operations. It's crucial to verify that backups are clean and that systems are functioning properly before bringing them back online. Additionally, monitor the systems closely for signs of re-infection.

**VI. Lessons Learned:** After the incident is over, conduct a post-incident review to evaluate the effectiveness of the response. Determine what was successful and what needs improvement. This review should be documented and used to update the incident response plan for future incidents.

### e) Establish Incident Severity Levels

Not all cyberattacks are equal in terms of impact. Some may involve a minor breach of a non-critical system, while others may compromise sensitive customer data or bring operations to a halt. To ensure a proportional response, it's important to define different severity levels for incidents.

**For example:**

**Low Severity:** Limited impact, such as a phishing email or a non-critical system compromise. The response may involve simply containing the threat and monitoring for further issues.

**Medium Severity:** Moderate impact, such as malware affecting a few systems or unauthorized access to non-sensitive data. The response may involve containment, eradication, and restoring affected systems.

**High Severity:** Major impact, such as a ransomware attack or breach of sensitive customer data. A full-scale response is required, involving containment, eradication, recovery, and communication with external stakeholders.

Having these levels defined in advance ensures that the response is appropriate to the severity of the attack.

### 3. Testing and Improving the Plan

An incident response plan is only as good as its execution. To ensure that your plan is effective, it must be regularly tested and updated. Conducting tabletop exercises, where the incident response team simulates a cyberattack, is an excellent way to practice and identify any gaps in the plan.

Additionally, after each real incident, conduct a thorough review to identify lessons learned. This helps improve the plan for future incidents and ensures that the organization continues to evolve its cybersecurity posture.

## 4. The Role of Cyber Insurance

While a robust incident response plan is critical, cyber insurance can also play a role in minimizing the financial impact of a cyberattack. Cyber insurance policies typically cover costs associated with data breaches, business interruption, and reputational damage. However, it's important to note that insurance should not be relied upon as a substitute for strong cybersecurity practices. Instead, it should be seen as a complementary tool to help manage the aftermath of an attack.

## 5. Conclusion: The Inevitable Will Happen – Be Prepared

In today's digital landscape, cyberattacks are inevitable. But by building a robust incident response plan, organizations can minimize the damage and recover swiftly. Cyber resilience is not just about preventing attacks but preparing for them. By understanding the importance of a well-defined incident response plan, testing it regularly, and continuously improving it, organizations can ensure that they are ready to face the inevitable with confidence.

A resilient organization is one that doesn't just survive a cyberattack but emerges stronger, more informed, and better equipped to handle future threats. In the end, it's not about avoiding cyberattacks altogether—it's about being prepared to bounce back quickly and effectively when they occur.

# Chapter 6: Guardians of the Grid: Safeguarding Critical Infrastructure

In the modern world, critical infrastructure forms the backbone of society, supporting everything from energy distribution to transportation networks, healthcare systems, and financial services. These essential services are not only the lifeblood of daily life but also the foundation of national security and economic stability. As our reliance on digital technologies increases, so does the vulnerability of these infrastructures to cyber threats. This chapter delves into the unique challenges faced in safeguarding critical infrastructure from cyberattacks and explores the solutions that can help protect these vital systems.

## The Growing Threat Landscape

Critical infrastructure is composed of systems and assets that are essential to the functioning of a nation's economy, security, and public health. These include energy grids, water treatment plants, transportation networks, telecommunications, and healthcare facilities. In the past, these systems were largely isolated from the internet, making them less susceptible to cyber threats. However, the increasing trend toward digitization, automation, and interconnectivity has made these systems more accessible and more vulnerable to cyberattacks.

Cyberattacks targeting critical infrastructure have become a significant concern for governments, businesses, and citizens alike. The threat landscape is evolving rapidly, with cybercriminals, hacktivists, and even state-sponsored actors using sophisticated tactics to disrupt essential services. These attacks can range from data breaches and ransomware attacks to more destructive forms of cyber warfare, such as the manipulation of industrial control systems (ICS) or the deployment of malware that can damage physical infrastructure.

The consequences of such attacks are severe. A successful cyberattack on critical infrastructure can lead to widespread service disruptions, economic losses, damage to public safety, and even loss of life. For example, a cyberattack on a power grid could cause blackouts that affect millions of people, while an attack on a water treatment facility could lead to contamination of drinking water. The increasing interconnectedness of systems only amplifies the potential for cascading failures, where an attack on one sector can have ripple effects across others.

## The Unique Challenges of Protecting Critical Infrastructure

Protecting critical infrastructure from cyber threats presents several unique challenges, including:

### 1. Legacy Systems and Technology Gaps

Many critical infrastructure systems were designed before the advent of modern cybersecurity practices and digital technologies. These legacy systems often lack the robust security measures necessary to defend against today's sophisticated cyber threats. Updating or replacing these systems is a complex and costly process, and many organizations struggle to balance the need for security with the limitations of outdated technology.

Moreover, some systems were never intended to be connected to the internet or other networks, making them inherently vulnerable to cyberattacks. The integration of legacy systems with newer, more secure technologies can create gaps in security, leaving critical infrastructure exposed to exploitation.

## 2. **Complexity and Interdependence**

Critical infrastructure is highly complex and interdependent. A failure in one sector can have a domino effect on others. For example, a cyberattack on a transportation network could disrupt the delivery of goods and services, which in turn could impact the energy supply or healthcare services. This interconnectedness makes it difficult to isolate and contain cyber threats.

The complexity of modern infrastructure also means that there are numerous entry points for attackers to exploit. From industrial control systems to cloud-based services, the range of potential vulnerabilities is vast. Securing every component of these systems requires a multi-layered approach that takes into account the unique risks posed by each part of the infrastructure.

## 3. Shortage of Skilled Cybersecurity Professionals

The cybersecurity industry is facing a global shortage of skilled professionals, and this shortage is particularly pronounced in the field of critical infrastructure protection. Many organizations struggle to find and retain cybersecurity experts who have the specialized knowledge required to protect complex systems like industrial control systems and operational technology.

This shortage of talent makes it difficult for organizations to stay ahead of emerging threats and implement effective cybersecurity strategies. Additionally, the increasing sophistication of cyberattacks requires continuous training and development to ensure that cybersecurity professionals can effectively respond to new and evolving threats.

## 4. Regulatory and Compliance Challenges

Governments around the world have recognized the importance of protecting critical infrastructure and have enacted various regulations and frameworks to address cybersecurity risks. However, these regulations often vary by country and sector, creating challenges for organizations that operate across borders or within multiple industries. Compliance with these regulations can be time-consuming and costly, especially for smaller organizations with limited resources.

Moreover, the rapidly changing nature of cyber threats means that regulations and compliance standards must evolve constantly. Organizations must be agile in adapting to new requirements, and failure to do so can result in significant penalties or reputational damage.

## 5. **The Risk of Insider Threats**

Insider threats pose a significant challenge to the security of critical infrastructure. Employees, contractors, or other trusted individuals with access to sensitive systems can intentionally or unintentionally compromise security. Insider threats can range from employees leaking sensitive information to malicious actors deliberately sabotaging systems.

The risk of insider threats is particularly high in sectors where employees have access to critical systems, such as energy grids, water treatment plants, and healthcare facilities. Addressing this threat requires a combination of robust access controls, monitoring systems, and employee training to reduce the likelihood of insider incidents.

## **Solutions for Protecting Critical Infrastructure**

While the challenges of protecting critical infrastructure from cyber threats are significant, there are several strategies and solutions that can help mitigate these risks:

## 1. Modernizing Legacy Systems

One of the most effective ways to improve the cybersecurity of critical infrastructure is to modernize legacy systems. This involves upgrading outdated technologies and integrating them with modern cybersecurity tools and practices. While this can be a costly and time-consuming process, it is essential for reducing vulnerabilities and ensuring that critical infrastructure can withstand modern cyber threats.

In some cases, it may not be feasible to replace legacy systems entirely. In these situations, organizations can implement security measures such as network segmentation, encryption, and firewalls to create additional layers of protection around vulnerable systems.

## 2. Implementing Multi-Layered Security

A multi-layered security approach is essential for protecting critical infrastructure from cyberattacks. This approach involves using a combination of technologies, processes, and policies to create multiple barriers to entry for attackers. For example, organizations can use firewalls, intrusion detection systems, and endpoint protection tools to defend against external threats, while also implementing access controls and monitoring systems to detect and respond to insider threats.

Industrial control systems and operational technology (OT) are particularly vulnerable to cyberattacks, and securing these systems requires specialized tools and techniques. Implementing network segmentation, ensuring that OT systems are isolated from corporate IT networks, and regularly patching vulnerabilities are critical steps in securing these systems.

## 3. Enhancing Collaboration and Information Sharing

Collaboration between government agencies, private sector organizations, and cybersecurity experts is essential for improving the security of critical infrastructure. Information sharing is particularly important in the context of emerging threats, as it allows organizations to learn from each other's experiences and stay ahead of cybercriminals.

Governments can play a key role in fostering collaboration by providing platforms for information sharing, offering incentives for organizations to report cybersecurity incidents, and developing public-private partnerships to address common threats.

## 4. Investing in Cybersecurity Training and Awareness

As the cybersecurity landscape continues to evolve, it is crucial to invest in training and awareness programs for employees at all levels of an organization. This includes not only cybersecurity professionals but also general staff who may inadvertently become the target of phishing attacks or other social engineering tactics.

Training should focus on both technical skills and the human aspects of cybersecurity, such as recognizing suspicious activity and understanding the potential consequences of cyberattacks. Regular exercises and simulations can help employees stay prepared for real-world cyber threats.

## 5. **Strengthening Incident Response and Recovery Plans**

No cybersecurity strategy is foolproof, and there is always a risk that an attack will breach an organization's defenses. Therefore, it is essential to have robust incident response and recovery plans in place. These plans should outline the steps to take in the event of a cyberattack, including how to contain the attack, communicate with stakeholders, and recover affected systems.

Testing and updating incident response plans regularly is essential to ensure that they remain effective. Additionally, organizations should implement backup systems and disaster recovery protocols to minimize downtime and restore critical services as quickly as possible.

## **Conclusion**

As the guardians of the grid, those tasked with protecting critical infrastructure face a complex and ever-evolving landscape of cyber threats. The challenges are significant, but with the right strategies and solutions, it is possible to safeguard these essential services from cyberattacks. Modernizing legacy systems, implementing multi-layered security, fostering collaboration, investing in training, and strengthening incident response plans are all key components of a comprehensive cybersecurity strategy.

In an increasingly digital world, the protection of critical infrastructure is not just a technical challenge, it is a matter of national security, economic stability, and public safety. By adopting a proactive and collaborative approach, we can ensure that these vital systems remain resilient in the face of ever-growing cyber threats.

# Chapter 7: Future-Proofing Cybersecurity: Trends and Technologies to Watch

As the digital landscape continues to evolve at a rapid pace, cybersecurity must evolve in tandem to address new threats and challenges. The future of cybersecurity is not just about responding to attacks, but about anticipating and mitigating potential risks before they can cause harm. This chapter explores the emerging trends and technologies that will shape the cybersecurity landscape in the years to come, offering insights into how businesses and individuals can stay ahead of the curve.

**1. The Rise of Artificial Intelligence and Machine Learning in Cybersecurity**

Artificial Intelligence (AI) and Machine Learning (ML) have already begun to revolutionize many industries, and cybersecurity is no exception. AI and ML are increasingly being used to detect, prevent, and respond to cyber threats with greater speed and accuracy than ever before.

**AI-Powered Threat Detection:** One of the most promising applications of AI in cybersecurity is its ability to detect anomalies and potential threats in real time. By analyzing vast amounts of data, AI can identify patterns that may indicate malicious activity, such as unusual login times or abnormal data access patterns. This allows for faster identification of potential breaches and more effective responses.

**Automated Response and Incident Management:** AI can also automate many of the manual processes involved in cybersecurity incident response. For example, AI-driven systems can automatically isolate infected systems, block malicious traffic, and even initiate countermeasures without human intervention. This reduces response times and minimizes the impact of a breach.

**Predictive Analytics:** Machine learning algorithms can analyze historical data to predict potential future threats. By understanding how cybercriminals operate and learning from past incidents, AI and ML can help organizations proactively defend against emerging threats, giving them a critical edge in the battle against cybercrime.

## 2. Quantum Computing and Its Implications for Cybersecurity

Quantum computing, which leverages the principles of quantum mechanics, is poised to revolutionize the field of cybersecurity. While quantum computers are still in the early stages of development, their potential to break traditional encryption methods has raised significant concerns.

**Quantum-Resistant Cryptography:** One of the most pressing concerns with the advent of quantum computing is its ability to crack current encryption algorithms, such as RSA and ECC (Elliptic Curve Cryptography), which form the backbone of most modern cybersecurity protocols. Quantum computers could potentially solve complex mathematical problems, like factoring large numbers, much faster than classical computers, rendering many of today's encryption methods obsolete.

In response, researchers are developing quantum-resistant cryptographic algorithms that are designed to withstand the computational power of quantum machines. These algorithms are expected to become a critical part of cybersecurity in the coming years, ensuring that sensitive data remains secure even in a quantum-powered world.

**Post-Quantum Cryptography:** As quantum computing becomes more advanced, organizations will need to adopt post-quantum cryptographic techniques. This involves transitioning to encryption methods that are resistant to the capabilities of quantum computers, ensuring that data remains protected in the long term. Governments and industries are already beginning to invest heavily in post-quantum cryptography research to prepare for the inevitable arrival of quantum computing.

## 3. Zero Trust Architecture: A Paradigm Shift in Security

Zero Trust Architecture (ZTA) is rapidly becoming a foundational principle in modern cybersecurity strategies. The traditional model of perimeter-based security, where trust is granted based on network location, is increasingly inadequate in a world where remote work, cloud computing, and mobile devices are the norm.

**Never Trust, Always Verify:** The core principle of Zero Trust is that no user or device, whether inside or outside the network, should be trusted by default. Every access request is treated as potentially malicious, and access is granted based on strict identity verification, continuous monitoring, and least-privilege access principles. This approach ensures that even if an attacker gains access to a network, they will be severely limited in what they can do.

**Identity and Access Management (IAM):** Zero Trust relies heavily on robust Identity and Access Management (IAM) systems. These systems use multi-factor authentication (MFA), biometric verification, and other advanced techniques to ensure that only authorized users and devices can access critical systems and data.

**Micro-Segmentation:** Another key aspect of Zero Trust is micro-segmentation, which involves dividing networks into smaller, isolated segments to limit the movement of potential attackers. Even if an attacker manages to breach one segment, they will be unable to access other parts of the network without additional authentication.

4. **Blockchain Technology:** Enhancing Data Integrity and Transparency

Blockchain, the decentralized ledger technology behind cryptocurrencies like Bitcoin, is increasingly being explored for its potential to enhance cybersecurity. Its inherent characteristics of decentralization, immutability, and transparency make it a promising solution for various cybersecurity challenges.

**Decentralized Identity Management:** Blockchain can be used to create decentralized identity management systems, where individuals control their own identity data. Instead of relying on centralized databases that can be hacked or manipulated, blockchain allows users to store and manage their identity securely. This reduces the risk of identity theft and fraud.

**Data Integrity and Tamper-Proof Logs:** Blockchain's immutable nature ensures that once data is recorded, it cannot be altered or deleted without detection. This makes it an ideal solution for securing logs and ensuring data integrity. For example, blockchain can be used to create tamper-proof logs of network activity, making it easier to detect and investigate cyberattacks.

**Smart Contracts for Security Automation:** Blockchain-based smart contracts can be used to automate various cybersecurity processes, such as access control and compliance checks. These contracts are self-executing and can automatically enforce security policies without human intervention, reducing the risk of human error.

## 5. <u>5G Networks and the Expanding Attack Surface</u>

The rollout of 5G networks is expected to bring about significant advancements in speed, connectivity, and IoT (Internet of Things) integration. However, it also introduces new cybersecurity challenges that organizations must address.

**Increased Attack Surface:** The widespread adoption of 5G will connect billions of new devices to the internet, creating a much larger attack surface for cybercriminals to exploit. With the rise of connected devices, such as smart home systems, wearables, and industrial IoT devices, the potential for cyberattacks increases exponentially.

**Network Slicing and Security:** 5G networks use a technology called network slicing, which allows different virtual networks to be created within a single physical network. While this offers greater flexibility and efficiency, it also introduces new security risks. Each network slice must be properly secured to prevent attackers from gaining access to sensitive data or critical infrastructure.

**Securing the IoT Ecosystem:** The explosion of IoT devices in a 5G world means that securing these devices will become even more important. Many IoT devices have weak security, making them vulnerable to exploitation. Ensuring that these devices are secure and can be properly monitored will be a key challenge in the 5G era.

## 6. Cloud Security and the Shift to Hybrid Environments

As more businesses move their operations to the cloud, securing cloud environments has become a top priority. However, with the increasing complexity of hybrid cloud environments where organizations use a mix of on-premises, private, and public cloud services ensuring comprehensive security is more challenging than ever.

**Cloud-Native Security:** Cloud-native security tools are being developed to address the unique challenges of securing cloud environments. These tools provide visibility into cloud workloads, monitor for potential threats, and automatically respond to incidents in real time.

**Hybrid Cloud Security:** As organizations adopt hybrid cloud strategies, they must ensure that their security solutions work seamlessly across both on-premises and cloud environments. This requires integrated security solutions that can monitor and protect data, applications, and infrastructure across multiple platforms.

**Data Privacy and Compliance:** With the increasing amount of data being stored in the cloud, ensuring compliance with data privacy regulations (such as GDPR) is critical. Cloud service providers and organizations must work together to implement strong data protection measures and ensure that sensitive information is kept secure.

## 7. Cybersecurity Automation and Orchestration

As cyber threats become more sophisticated and frequent, manual processes are no longer sufficient to keep up with the volume of potential attacks. Cybersecurity automation and orchestration are emerging as critical tools for organizations to streamline their security operations and respond more effectively to threats.

**Automated Threat Detection and Response:** Automation can help organizations detect and respond to threats faster by reducing the time it takes to identify and mitigate risks. For example, automated systems can instantly analyze incoming traffic, identify potential threats, and take action such as blocking malicious IP addresses or quarantining infected files without human intervention.

**Security Orchestration:** Security orchestration involves integrating multiple security tools and systems to work together in a coordinated manner. This allows organizations to automate complex workflows, such as incident response and threat hunting, ensuring that security teams can respond to incidents more efficiently.

**Reducing Human Error:** By automating routine tasks, organizations can reduce the risk of human error, which is often a major cause of security breaches. Automation can help ensure that security processes are consistently followed and that threats are addressed in a timely manner.

To conclude ;

The future of cybersecurity is shaped by a combination of emerging technologies, evolving threats, and changing business needs. To stay ahead of the curve, organizations must embrace new tools and strategies, such as AI and ML, quantum-resistant cryptography, Zero Trust, blockchain, and cloud-native security solutions. By doing so, they can build a resilient cybersecurity framework that is capable of addressing both current and future threats. As the digital landscape continues to evolve, future-proofing cybersecurity will require constant vigilance, innovation, and adaptation to new technologies and trends.

# Appendix

## Appendix A: Cybersecurity Glossary

A comprehensive glossary of key terms and jargon used in cybersecurity, such as:

**Zero-Day Exploit:** A software vulnerability unknown to the vendor.

**Phishing:** Fraudulent attempts to obtain sensitive information by disguising as a trustworthy entity.

**Encryption:** The process of converting information into a secure format.

This section helps readers quickly understand technical terms encountered in the book.

## Appendix B: Essential Tools and Resources

A curated list of tools, websites, and platforms for enhancing cybersecurity, categorized by function:

**Antivirus and Malware Protection:** Bitdefender, Norton, Malwarebytes.
**Password Managers:** LastPass, Dashlane, 1Password.
**Network Monitoring Tools:** Wireshark, SolarWinds.

**Educational Resources:**
Cybersecurity blogs like Krebs on Security.
Online courses on platforms like Coursera and Udemy.

## Appendix C: Incident Response Checklist

A step-by-step guide for individuals and organizations to follow during a cybersecurity breach:

**1. Identify the Breach:** Analyze logs and alerts to confirm the incident.
**2. Contain the Threat:** Disconnect affected systems from the network.
**3. Eradicate the Issue:** Remove malware or compromised accounts.
**4. Recover Systems:** Restore from clean backups.
**5. Learn and Improve:** Conduct a post-mortem analysis to prevent future breaches.

## Appendix D: Cybersecurity Regulations and Standards

Summarize key laws and frameworks:

**GDPR (General Data Protection Regulation):** Applicable to organizations handling EU citizen data.
**HIPAA (Health Insurance Portability and Accountability Act):** Protects healthcare data.
**ISO/IEC 27001:** A global standard for information security management systems.
Include practical tips for compliance.

## Appendix E: Case Studies: Learning from Real-Life Incidents

Briefly describe notable cybersecurity incidents and the lessons learned:

**Target Data Breach (2013):** Caused by a third-party vendor's compromised credentials.
Lesson: Ensure vendor security practices are robust.
**WannaCry Ransomware (2017):** Exploited unpatched systems.
**Lesson:** Regularly update and patch software.

## Appendix F: Top Cybersecurity Tips for Everyday Users

Quick, actionable advice for readers:

Use multi-factor authentication (MFA) for all accounts.

Avoid public Wi-Fi for sensitive transactions.

Regularly backup important data to a secure location.

## **Appendix G: Future Trends in Cybersecurity**

Provide insights into emerging technologies and threats:

- AI-driven cyber attacks and defenses.
- Quantum computing's impact on encryption.
- The rise of IoT vulnerabilities.

www.ingramcontent.com/pod-product-compliance
Lightning Source LLC
Chambersburg PA
CBHW071101240526
45471CB00016B/2300